Are Trees Alive?

Debbie S. Miller

Illustrations by Stacey Schuett

SCHOLASTIC INC.
New York Toronto London Auckland Sydney
Mexico City New Delhi Hong Kong Buenos Aires

For my daughter, Casey,
with love
—D. M.

For Clare and Ian,
who want to know
—S. S.

Many thanks to all the
foresters, botanists, and naturalists
who provided information about the trees
described in this book.

The art was created with acrylic paint and gouache on Arches watercolor paper.
Book design by Diane Hobbing of Snap-Haus Graphics.

Text copyright © 2002 by Debbie S. Miller.
Illustrations copyright © 2002 by Stacy Schuett.
All rights reserved. Published by Scholastic Inc., 557 Broadway, New York, NY 10012,
by arrangement with Walker & Company.
Printed in the U.S.A.

ISBN 0-439-85194-7

SCHOLASTIC and associated logos and designs are
trademarks and/or registered trademarks of Scholastic Inc.

6 7 8 9 10   40   13 12 11 10 09

Introduction

One day I hiked near a forest with my four-year-old daughter, Casey. She looked up at a tall spruce tree and asked, "Are trees alive?" I answered yes and explained that trees were living things. She responded, "But how do they breathe; they don't have noses?"

Her question inspired me to look closely at the features of trees and compare them to humans. Although trees are plants and humans are animals, we have many similar characteristics. This book describes those characteristics, and celebrates some of the magnificent trees that grow on our planet, along with the diversity of life that surrounds them. Trees are special. They are fun to climb and dream beneath. They shade us on hot summer days. They release oxygen for us to breathe. They drop beautiful autumn leaves. They give us fruits, wood, paper, medicines, and foods like chocolate and maple syrup. They provide habitat for countless animals. They help clean pollution from the air. When you walk through a forest, take a close look at the trees around you, and say thank you.

Remember to treat trees with respect, use them wisely, and recycle.

Plant a Tree

Each year more and more trees are cut down. After you read this book, find a good place to plant a tree with your family or class. Give your tree a special name, watch it grow, and see what kind of animals visit it. If you send me a digital picture of your tree, I'll place it in a tree photo album on my Web site. I wonder how many different trees will be planted? How many animals will find a new home? Visit my Web site at www.debbiemilleralaska.com for more information.

To learn more about planting trees in your state visit the National Arbor Day Foundation's Web site at: www.arborday.org

Long roots wiggle through the soil. They gather water and minerals that trees need to grow. Roots anchor a tree, like your feet help you stand.

Sturdy trunks stand short and tall. A trunk supports
the body of a tree, like your legs support your body.

Branches hold animals, the nests of birds, swings, and tree houses. They sway gently in the wind, like a mother's arms rocking a baby.

Bark is dark or light, rough or smooth, thick or thin, just like people's skin. Bark protects the inside of a tree from harsh weather and insects, like your skin protects you.

The crown of a tree reaches for the sky and gathers sunlight. A crown is at the top of a tree, like your head is at the top of your body. The branches and leaves of a large crown give you lots of shade on a hot summer day.

Leaves breathe for the tree. Trees need air just like you need air. Instead of using noses and lungs, leaves breathe through thousands of tiny pores known as stomata. Leaves flutter in the breeze like your hair blows in the wind.

Sticky sap travels through small tubes inside the tree, between the roots and the leaves. Without sap, the tree could not live, just like your body could not live without blood. Look at the veins in a leaf and compare them to the veins in your hand. Some tree sap is harvested by people.

Trees grow flowers of all shapes and sizes, of bright and soft colors. A pretty flower can attract insects and birds, just like your smiling face can attract a new friend. Animals feed on the nectar and pollen of the flowers. They help spread the pollen so that trees can make seeds and grow fruits.

Some seeds are tiny and fluffy and fly with the wind. Others are protected inside their fruit. The coconut tree grows the largest seed on Earth. Seeds sprout and become saplings, then grow up to be trees. Just like babies become children, then grow up to be adults.

Some trees die because of fires, disease, or storm damage. Many trees are cut down by people for their wood. But some trees live to be very, very old, just like some people live more than 100 years.

During winter some trees have bare limbs and twigs that lace the cold sky. This is the time when many trees rest without their leaves. Trees rest too, just like you.

When spring comes, the trees awaken from their winter's rest. Leaf buds swell on the branches. Cherry trees blossom. With more sunshine the trees burst with new life, just like you burst out the door with your friends to play and celebrate spring.

While you picnic under a tree, the forest has a picnic of its own. The sun helps the leaves make food, the rain brings drink, and the wind brings music to the forest.

Steller's jay

African elephant

baboon

About the Trees

black-tailed deer

Baobab Tree of Africa *Adansonia digitata*

There are a number of African folktales about the baobab tree, also known as "the upside-down tree." One story describes a hyena that accidentally planted the baobab tree upside down, and this explains why its branches look like twisted roots. During rainy periods, the baobab's shallow roots absorb as much water as possible. The massive trunks have spongy wood that can store as much as 25,000 gallons of water, enough to fill about 625 bathtubs!

Scattered across Africa's savanna, these trees provide habitat for animals such as yellow-billed hornbills, baboons, and elephants. African people eat the baobab fruit, collect honey from hives within the trunk, make rope from its bark, and use the roots and leaves for medicine.

spotted owl

Coast Redwood Tree of California and Oregon *Sequoia sempervirens*

The majestic coast redwood lives in foggy, moist areas along the coast of California and Oregon. This evergreen grows taller than any other tree in the world—some redwoods reach heights of nearly 370 feet. That's as high as a thirty-seven-story building. The coast redwood is a long-lived tree and can grow for more than 2,000 years.

Redwoods provide shade for ferns and mosses. At dusk, animals such as the endangered spotted owl and black-tailed deer feed in the redwood forest. During the day, listen for the noisy call of the Steller's jay.

koala

Ribbon Gum Tree of Australia *Eucalyptus viminalis*

The ribbon gum, also known as the manna gum, is one of 500 species of eucalyptus trees that grow in Australia. The leaves of the ribbon gum are a favorite food of the koala. Yellow-bellied sugar gliders eat the gummy sap beneath the bark of the trunk and branches. Birds, such as the kookaburra and the roseate cockatoo, can be spotted in the ribbon gum.

The wood of the ribbon gum is used for building, flooring, and paneling.

kookaburra

Paper Birch of North America *Betula papyrifera*

The paper birch has beautiful white bark that grows in paper-thin layers. Native American people had many uses for this water-resistant bark. Northeast tribes used it to make food containers, baskets, wigwam coverings, and canoes. A 17-foot birch bark canoe was light enough to be carried by one person, yet it could hold up to 1,000 pounds.

Today, Alaska's Athabaskan Indians continue to make baskets, bowls, and other items out of birch bark. Many animals depend on Alaska's northern forest, such as hairy woodpeckers and moose, the largest deer in the world. There are many types of birch throughout the Northern Hemisphere.

sugar glider

roseate cockatoo

moose

hairy woodpecker

yellow-billed hornbill

deer mouse

Banyan Tree of India *Ficus benghalensis*

The banyan tree is considered sacred to many people in India. This tree has the biggest crown of any tree in the world. A banyan tree is often located in the center of a village or town. The tree has many spreading branches that send out aerial roots. When the roots reach the ground, they turn into pillars that help support the huge branches. When you walk in the shade of a banyan tree, you feel like you are walking in a forest. A single banyan tree can shade as much as five acres of land, about the size of four football fields.

red fox
kit

Weeping Willow of China *Salix babylonica*

The weeping willow has long, thin branches that cascade to the ground. Originating in China and central Asia, the weeping willow is one of the first trees to show green in the spring. Weeping willow leaves are different than those of other trees. Most trees have tiny breathing pores, or stomata, on the underside of their leaves. Willows have stomata on both sides. Each stoma is about the size of a pinprick.

   There are about 300 species of willows that grow on Earth. Willows are an important source of food and shelter for many animals. The bark and leaves of willows were used by people in early times to relieve pain. Willows contain salicin, the source of aspirin.

emerald tree boa

Sugar Maple of Canada *Acer saccharum*

The sugar maple is Canada's national emblem. A red maple leaf appears on the country's flag. Sugar maples are spectacular during autumn when the leaves turn brilliant colors. Maples are tapped for their sugar. One sugar maple might produce as much as 40 gallons of sap. It takes about 35 to 40 gallons of sap to make one gallon of pure maple syrup. As temperatures warm in late winter, the sap begins to run up the sapwood of the tree. This is when people drain some of the sap into buckets.

bee

Cocoa and Kapok Trees of South America *Theobroma cacao* and *Ceiba pentandra*

The cocoa tree, or chocolate tree, produces big fruit pods that each contain as many as 60 seeds. The seeds are roasted and ground into cocoa powder. It takes about 400 seeds to make one pound of pure chocolate!

   Kapok trees produce long, leathery fruits with seeds that are contained in thick masses of cottonlike fibers. The fibers, known as kapok, are used to stuff pillows, mattresses, and toys. The kapok tree is one of the tallest trees in the rain forest. At night the white flowers of the kapok tree open, and nocturnal bats feed on the nectar.

fruit bat

red squirrel

blue morpho butterfly

white-tailed tropic bird

least chipmunk

raven

magnificent frigate bird

western gray squirrel

ruffed grouse

black bear

mountain bluebird

common porcupine

beaver

snowshoe hare

Double Coconut Tree of the Seychelles *Lodoicea maldivica*

The double coconut tree is also known as the coco-de-mer palm tree. This tree grows the biggest seed in the world. Each coconut contains two fruits and weighs as much as fifty pounds, the same weight as an average six-year-old child. The tough shells of coconuts enable them to float at sea and find new land in which to take root.

Coconut trees have many important uses. The long leaves are used as thatch (roof cover), and they are woven into baskets, hats, or mats. The raffia palm of Africa grows the longest leaves in the world. One leaf can measure 25 yards, as long as a standard swimming pool! The fruit, milk, and oil of coconuts are widely used.

Bristlecone Pine of western America *Pinus aristata*

Bristlecone pines grow very slowly and are the oldest living things on Earth. One tree in the Ancient Bristlecone Forest of eastern California is nearly 4,800 years old. When this tree was a seedling, the Egyptians were building pyramids!

Bristlecone pines grow at high elevations and are often lashed by the wind and covered with snow and ice. Their trunks are twisted and gnarled. Bristlecone pines can be found in several western states. The least chipmunk and raven are common residents of the bristle-cone forest.

Major Oak of Sherwood Forest, England *Quercus robur*

Major Oak is a magnificent English oak tree in Sherwood Forest. This giant tree weighs an estimated 23 tons and is more than 800 years old. The legendary Robin Hood may have hid from his enemies inside this famous tree.

Major Oak has a large hollow interior caused by fungi growth. The hollow provides good winter habitat for hibernating insects and mammals such as butterflies, spiders, and bats. Major Oak produces many thousands of acorns that are an important food source for squirrels, deer, and other animals. Many people from all over the world visit this ancient tree each year.

Cherry Tree of Japan *Prunus serrulata*

The cherry tree is the national tree of Japan. White and pink blossomed cherry trees can be seen throughout the country. There are at least 60 different varieties of this beautiful flowering tree. The cherry tree signifies the arrival of spring, and the Japanese celebrate by holding a cherry blossom festival in April. Families gather outside for picnics and sing songs. Artists share their work, which shows the beauty of the cherry blossoms.

Quaking Aspen of North America *Populus tremuloides*

Quaking aspen trees can be found throughout most of North America. With the softest breeze, the round-shaped leaves create a whisper of music. The leaves quake easily because each leaf's stem is flattened at a right angle to the leaf. The leaf pivots on the stem with the slightest movement of air.

One aspen forest in Utah is thought to be the largest living organism on Earth. More than 100 acres of aspen trees share the same root system, which originates from one male tree. As the roots spread they send up shoots to start new trees. Each tree is an identical clone of the father tree. Aspen buds and bark are an important food for snowshoe hare, moose, black bear, rabbits, porcupine, grouse, beaver, and deer.